The Good Father
Luke 15: God is Patient

CATHERINE MACKENZIE
Illustrated by Chiara Bertelli

CF4•K
Learn it: God is patient and merciful
Do it: Love God first. Love others.
Find it: What does God want? 2 Peter 3:9

Who would you ask to a party? Would it be friends or people that you'd like to be your friends? Would you ask girls and boys that nobody liked?

Some people turned up their noses at Jesus because he ate with people who did wrong things. They didn't realise that they did wrong things too.

Those people thought they were better than others. So Jesus told them a story about a young son, his older brother and their loving father.

The younger son said to his father, 'Give me my share of your money.' The father divided his wealth between his two sons. Then the younger son left home and went to a far country.

Soon he had wasted all his money. Poor and hungry, he had to get a job working with pigs. The young man realised how foolish he had been.

My father's hired men have plenty to eat,' he said. So the young man chose to return home. 'I'll ask my father to make me his servant,' he decided.

With that, the young man got up and returned home. But while he was still a long way off, his father saw him. He ran towards his son and gave him a big hug.

Before the young son could apologise properly, the father ordered the servants to treat his son like a prince.

'Dress him in the best robe. Put a ring on his finger. Get some sandals for his feet. And let's have a huge celebration! My son was dead and has come back to life again! He was lost and is found.'

Everyone began to be merry. But when the oldest son heard the news, he refused to join the party.

He complained to his father, 'I have served you for so long. I always obeyed you, but you never even had a dinner for me! Now this son of yours has come back. He has wasted your wealth yet you have a huge celebration for him!'

The father replied gently, 'My child, you have always been with me, and all that is mine is yours. But we must rejoice for this brother of yours was dead and has begun to live. He was lost and now is found!'

What does Jesus want you to learn from this story?

Well, the younger son was sinful. But he realised this and returned to his father. We must come to God and ask him to forgive us. He will welcome us just as warmly as the father welcomed his young son.

The oldest son was sinful. Although he had worked hard, his heart was wrong. He didn't really love his father. He wasn't happy about obeying him.

You may not have sinned in the same way that others have — but you're still a sinner if you don't love God the best.

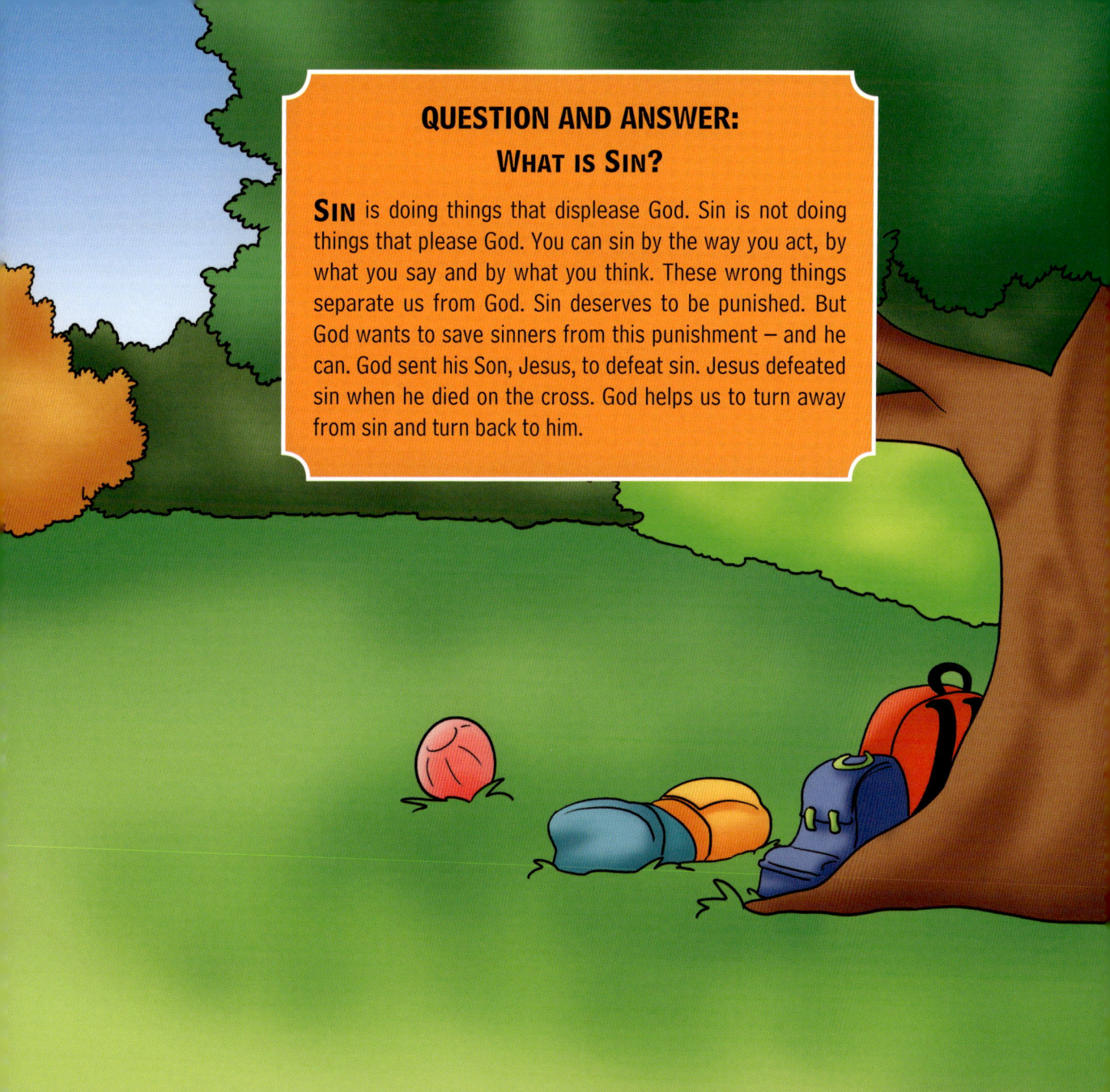

QUESTION AND ANSWER:
WHAT IS SIN?

SIN is doing things that displease God. Sin is not doing things that please God. You can sin by the way you act, by what you say and by what you think. These wrong things separate us from God. Sin deserves to be punished. But God wants to save sinners from this punishment — and he can. God sent his Son, Jesus, to defeat sin. Jesus defeated sin when he died on the cross. God helps us to turn away from sin and turn back to him.

We are all sinners. We all need God to forgive us. God is like the father in the story.

God is eager to forgive. We must accept the fact that we've sinned against God and go to him to ask for mercy.

God welcomes back sinners no matter what kind of sin they have done. Those who are wild and selfish, like the younger son, must repent.

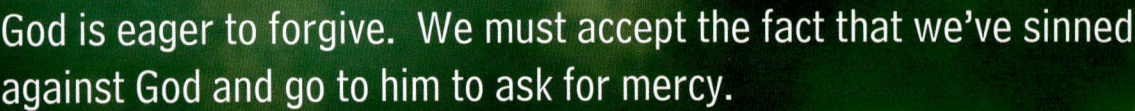

Those who are unloving and selfish like the older son must repent. God longs to welcome all types of sinners into his family.

Christian Focus Publications

Christian Focus Publications publishes books for adults and children under its four main imprints: Christian Focus, CF4K, Mentor and Christian Heritage. Our books reflect our conviction that God's Word is reliable and Jesus is the way to know him, and live for ever with him. Our children's list includes a Sunday School curriculum that covers pre-school to early teens, and puzzle and activity books. We also publish personal and family devotional titles, biographies and inspirational stories that children will love. If you are looking for quality Bible teaching for children then we have an excellent range of Bible stories and age-specific theological books. From pre-school board books to teenage apologetics, we have it covered!

AUTHOR'S DEDICATON: To my friends and family at Kingsview Christian Centre, A.P.C.

10 9 8 7 6 5 4 3 2 1

Copyright © 2016 Catherine Mackenzie

ISBN: 978-1-78191-753-4

Published in 2016 by Christian Focus Publications Ltd.
Geanies House, Fearn, Tain, Ross-shire, IV20 1TW, Great Britain

Illustrations by Chiara Bertelli
Cover Design: Sarah Bosman
Printed in China

All rights reserved. No part of this publication may be reproduced, stored in a retrieval system, or transmitted, in any form, by any means, electronic, mechanical, photocopying, recording or otherwise without the prior permission of the publisher or a licence permitting restricted copying. In the U.K. such licences are issued by the Copyright Licensing Agency, Saffron House, 6-10 Kirby Street, London, EC1 8TS. www.cla.co.uk

Scripture quotations are from The Holy Bible, English Standard Version, copyright © 2001 by Crossway Bibles, a division of Good News Publishers. Used by permission. All rights reserved. ESV Text Edition: 2007.